Wherever Wally goes, there are lots of other characters and lost things for you to spot. First find Wally, then look for Woof (but all you can see is his tail), Wenda, Wizard Whitebeard and Odlaw. Can you find the one scene where the gang is featured twice? *Clue: It's "picture" perfect!*

Can you also find Wally's key, Woof's bone, Wenda's camera, Wizard Whitebeard's scroll and Odlaw's binoculars in every scene?

That's not all! Dozens of Wally-watchers appear in this book

 (there is at least one in every scene but some scenes have many more!).

First published 2017 by Walker Books Ltd, 87 Vauxhall Walk, London SE11 5HJ • 2 4 6 8 10 9 7 5 3 1 • © 1987 – 2017 Martin Handford • The right of Martin Handford to be identified as author/illustrator of this work has been asserted by him in accordance with the Copyright, Designs and Patents Act 1988 • This book has been typeset in Optima and Wallyfont • Printed in China • All rights reserved. No part of this book may be reproduced, transmitted or stored in an information retrieval system in any form or by any means, graphic, electronic or mechanical, including photocopying, taping and recording, without prior written permission from the publisher. • British Library Cataloguing in Publication Data: a catalogue record for this book is available from the British Library • ISBN 978-1-4063-7624-1 • www.walker.co.uk

WHERE'S WALLY?

DESTINATION: EVERYWHERE!

MARTIN HANDFORD

WALKER BOOKS
AND SUBSIDIARIES
LONDON • BOSTON • SYDNEY • AUCKLAND

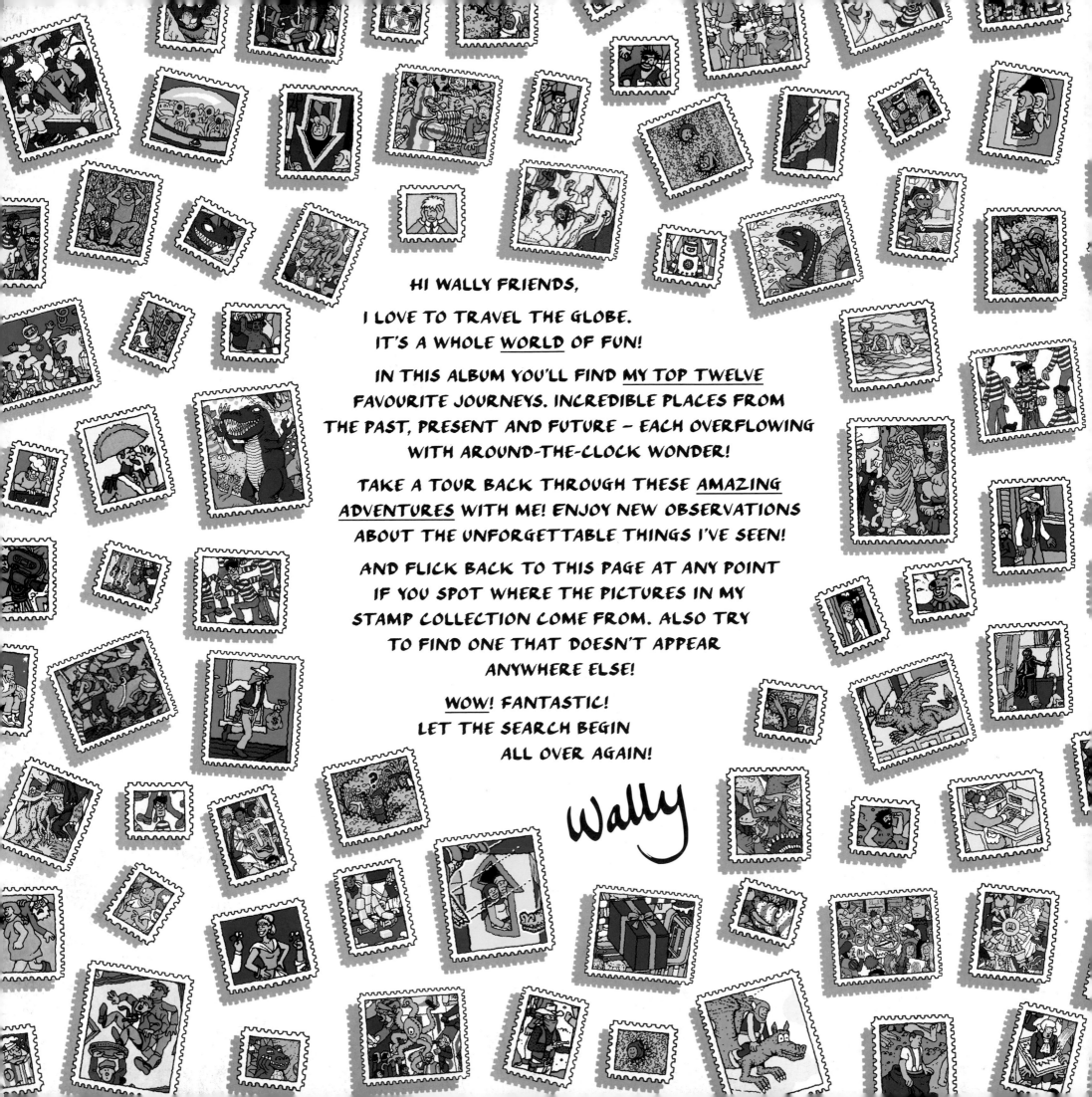

HI WALLY FRIENDS,

I LOVE TO TRAVEL THE GLOBE.
IT'S A WHOLE <u>WORLD</u> OF FUN!

IN THIS ALBUM YOU'LL FIND <u>MY TOP TWELVE</u>
FAVOURITE JOURNEYS. INCREDIBLE PLACES FROM
THE PAST, PRESENT AND FUTURE – EACH OVERFLOWING
WITH AROUND-THE-CLOCK WONDER!

TAKE A TOUR BACK THROUGH THESE <u>AMAZING</u>
<u>ADVENTURES</u> WITH ME! ENJOY NEW OBSERVATIONS
ABOUT THE UNFORGETTABLE THINGS I'VE SEEN!

AND FLICK BACK TO THIS PAGE AT ANY POINT
IF YOU SPOT WHERE THE PICTURES IN MY
STAMP COLLECTION COME FROM. ALSO TRY
TO FIND ONE THAT DOESN'T APPEAR
ANYWHERE ELSE!

<u>WOW!</u> FANTASTIC!
LET THE SEARCH BEGIN
ALL OVER AGAIN!

Wally

THE GREAT PORTRAIT EXHIBITION

I SAW SO MANY TERRIFIC THINGS WHEN I WANDERED AMONGST THE CROWDS AT THIS <u>ENORMOUS</u> EXHIBITION. ARTISTS MADE ART ALL OVER THE PLACE – ON WALLS, ON FLOORS AND ON PLANT POTS! GALLERY GAZERS ENJOYED EVERY TYPE OF PORTRAIT IMAGINABLE. I EVEN FOUND A PAINTING OF ME AND MY FRIENDS (BUT REMEMBER, WE'RE ALSO IN THE SCENE). CAN YOU FIND TWELVE DIFFERENCES BETWEEN THE LARGER SCENE AND THE SMALLER PICTURE ABOVE? ALSO SEE IF YOU CAN SPOT SOMETHING THAT, LIKE ME, CAN GO AND COME BACK AGAIN.* THIS EXHIBITION <u>NEVER CLOSES</u> SO KEEP ON SEARCHING!

*A BOOMERANG

PICTURE THIS

WOW! LOOK AT THESE <u>FANTASTIC</u> FRAMES! IN THEM ARE PORTRAITS OF PHENOMENAL PEOPLE AND CRAZY CREATURES FROM MY TRIPS TO <u>MANY</u> FAR-FLUNG DESTINATIONS. I LOVE THE PHOTOGRAPHS OF ME, MY FOUR FRIENDS, AND THE BOBBLE-HATTED WALLY-WATCHERS, TOO. DID YOU SPOT FOUR PICTURES THAT APPEAR TWICE IN THIS DAZZLING DISPLAY? HAVE YOU MATCHED THE SILHOUETTES IN THE FRAMES TO THE CHARACTERS WHO WANDERED OUT OF THEM? BUT THAT'S NOT ALL! MATCH THE PORTRAITS IN MY NEW COLLECTION ABOVE WITH THE MAIN SCENE TO REVEAL TWELVE THAT ARE FACING THE WRONG WAY. <u>INCREDIBLE!</u>

THE JURASSIC GAMES

GOODNESS CRETACEOUS, WHAT FRILLS THERE WERE TO SEE AT THE JURASSIC GAMES! THE EVENT WAS PACKED FULL OF SPECIMENS OF SPORT! I LOVED LISTENING TO THE ROARS AS ALL THE TEAMS PLAYED AT THE SAME TIME! BASH, CLASH, WALLOP! BONES AND ROCKS BOUNCED GALORE, OR WAS THAT THE SOUND OF HEADS CLASHING? I DID SEE REFEREES ... SOMEWHERE! SO MANY SPIKES, STRIPES, SPOTS AND SHARP TEETH! YIKES! NOW FIND WHERE THE PORTRAITS ABOVE COME FROM IN THE MAIN PICTURE – BUT BE WARNED, THE DINOSAURS HAVE CHANGED THEIR COLOURS!

ONCE UPON A PAGE...

YITSHOR	UMCSI
GACIM	YIRAF LSATE
TETREAILUR	TENVINSION
DOGO SEDED	MEGAS
SYEURNR	RAT

WHAT A WONDER IT WAS TO SEE BOOKS COME ALIVE AND CHARACTERS STEP OUT OF THEIR PAGES! I SAW TEEMING CROWDS OF FAMILIAR FACES FROM FOLKLORE SHARING THEIR FAVOURITE ADVENTURES. WOW! TERRIFIC! THERE WAS EVEN A BOOK ABOUT MY TRAVELS, WOOF'S BOOK OF ANIMAL STORIES, WENDA'S GUIDE TO ART, WIZARD WHITEBEARD'S BOOK OF MAGIC AND THE GREAT (BUT VERY SMALL!) BOOK OF ODLAW'S GOOD DEEDS. HA-HA! UNSCRAMBLE THE LETTERS ABOVE TO MAKE TEN WORDS! THEN FIND WHICH BOOKS PICTURED HAVE THOSE VERY WORDS IN THEIR TITLE! SPELLBINDING!

THE CAKE FACTORY

I'VE NEVER BEEN ANYWHERE AS DELICIOUS AS THE CAKE FACTORY. YUM! CHEFS WERE BUSY MAKING, BAKING AND DECORATING. IT HAD FLOORS UPON FLOORS OOZING WITH SCRUMPTIOUS SMELLS, TASTY TOPPINGS AND A MIXTURE OF CHAOS! HOW ABOUT THIS: FIND A WAY THROUGH THE TANGLED PIPES SO THE CHEF CAN TURN OFF THE DRIP-DRIP-DRIPPING TAP!

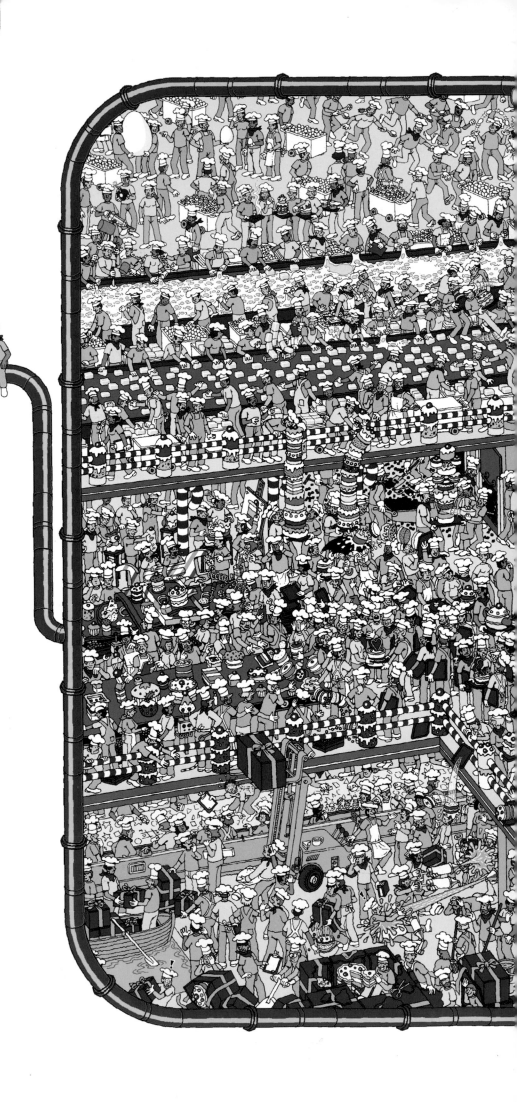

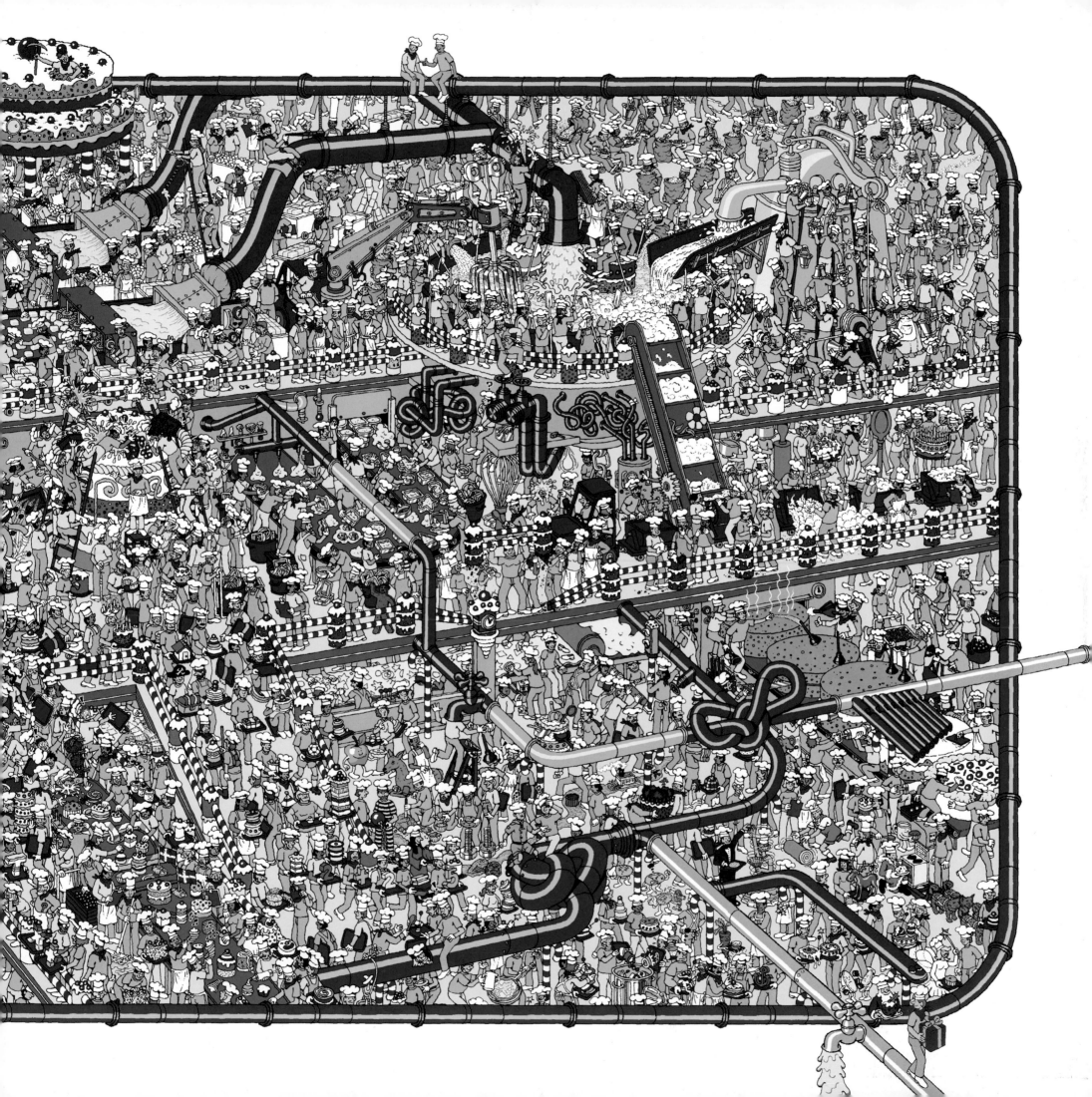

THE WILD WILD WEST

I ONCE SAW A WAGON TRAIN STEAM INTO TOWN ON A FANTASTIC FILM SET THAT LOOKED JUST LIKE THE AMERICAN WEST. IT WAS <u>WILD</u> AND <u>WACKY</u>! A COWBOY RODE OFF INTO A SUN "SET", A GOLD RUSH WAS IN FULL SWING AND A HORSE WORE REAL SHOES! HATS (AND SHOES!) OFF TO THEM! SPEAKING OF HATS, STUDY THE FIFTEEN CHARACTERS AT THE TOP OF THIS SIGN CLOSELY. ALL <u>BUT ONE</u> OF THEM HAVE SWAPPED THEIR HEADWEAR AROUND. FIRST, FIND THEM IN THE BIG PICTURE AND THEN FIGURE OUT WHO IS, AND WHO ISN'T, WEARING WHOSE HAT! <u>YEE-HA</u>!

THE GREAT ESCAPE

THIS WAS THE MOST **A-MAZE-ING** MAZE! THERE WERE TRAFFIC LIGHTS AND SIGNS POINTING IN EVERY DIRECTION! SOME PEOPLE WERE DIGGING AND CLIMBING TO ESCAPE, WHILE OTHERS FLEW BY BALLOON, BY SPRINGS AND EVEN BY ROCKET! I WONDER IF THE HOODED TEAMS EVER MADE IT OUT? DID <u>YOU</u> FIND A WAY FROM THE ENTRANCE TO THE EXIT? NOW TRY MY NEW CHAMPION CHALLENGE! CAN YOU FIND NOT JUST ONE, BUT TWO ROUTES THROUGH MY MOST MARVELLOUS MINI MAZE?

TOYS!
TOYS!
TOYS!

I'VE SEEN TOYS COME ALIVE WHEN THEY THOUGHT NO ONE WAS WATCHING. IT WAS MAGICAL! A TEDDY BEAR TOOK OFF FROM A BOOKSHELF IN A PAPER PLANE, A TOY ELEPHANT BLEW A SHIP'S SAIL WITH ITS TRUNK ... AND PLAYTIME AT THE TOY BOX WAS ONLY GETTING STARTED! SEE IF YOU CAN SOLVE MY SUPER SEQUENCE GAME SET IN THE RED AND YELLOW BUILDING BLOCKS ABOVE! FIND TEN SEQUENCES OF FIVE SYMBOLS THAT MATCH THOSE AROUND THE FRAME OF THIS BRILLIANTLY BUSY SCENE. THE SEQUENCES GO UP, DOWN, LEFT AND RIGHT!

PIRATE PANORAMA

ONE TIME I SAILED THE SEVEN SEAS WITH A BUNCH OF BARMY BUCCANEERS. AHOY! SOME OF THE PLUNDERING PIRATES I MET HAD PEG-LEGS, OTHERS HAD EYEPATCHES AND MANY WORE HATS WITH SKULL-AND-CROSSBONES! SHIVER ME TIMBERS! BUT THE CROSS ON THEIR TREASURE MAP REMAINED A MYSTERY. INSTEAD THEY HAD FUN FIRING CANNONS, STEALING SWAGGER FROM SHIPS AND MAKING LANDLUBBERS WALK THE PLANK! BOOM! SPLASH! YO-HO-HO! LOOK CLOSELY AT THE TEN JOLLY ROGER FLAGS FLYING UP ABOVE. CAN YOU SPOT THE TWO THAT MATCH? FOR A PIRATE TWIST, COVER ONE EYE WITH YOUR HAND AS YOU SEARCH!

THE DRAGON FLYERS

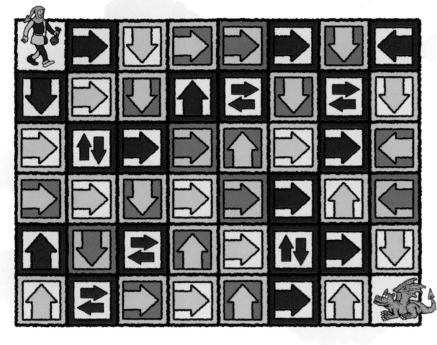

SNAP, SWOOP, CRASH! HAVE YOU EVER MET A DRAGON? <u>I DID</u>, IN THE LAND OF THE DRAGON FLYERS! THERE WERE CLUMSY FLEETS OF FLYING COLOURS AND ARROW SHAPES APLENTY TO SPOT IN THAT TERRIFIC TALE OF TAILS. NOW FIND A WAY THROUGH MY NEW MAZE! START AT THE MAN CLUTCHING A MONEYBAG AND FOLLOW THE DIRECTION OF THE ARROWS TO REACH THE DRAGON. SQUARES MUST TOUCH ONE ANOTHER AND NO DIAGONAL MOVES ALLOWED! IF YOU HIT A DEAD END, START AGAIN! <u>GOOD LUCK!</u>

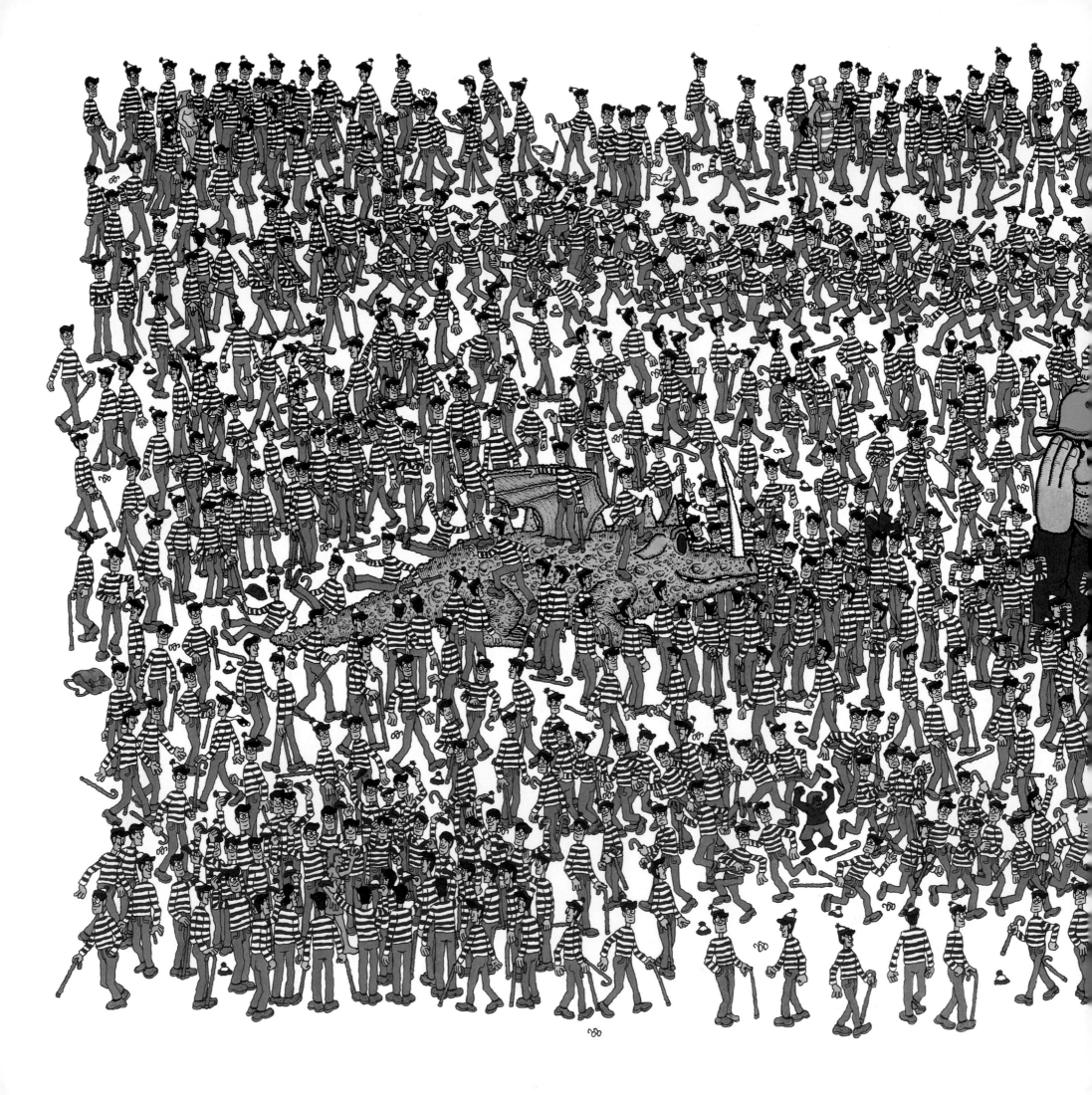

THE LAND OF WALLIES

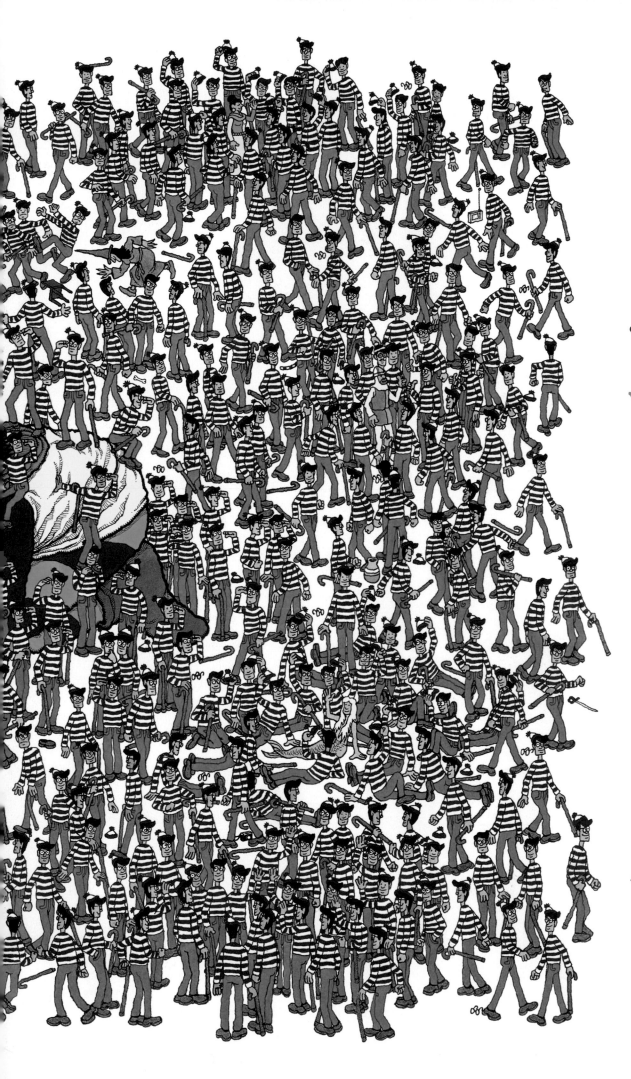

THE ULTIMATE SEARCH TO FIND ME WAS IN THE LAND OF WALLIES! WIZARD WHITEBEARD'S MULTIPLYING MAGIC MADE A MIRAGE OF RED-AND-WHITE STRIPED WANDERERS, AS WELL AS LOTS OF LOST WALKING STICKS, SPECTACLES AND BOBBLE HATS! BUT DID YOU FIND THE REAL ME? I HAD LOST A SHOE — DID YOU SPOT IT ANYWHERE? AND THERE WERE TEN OTHER CHARACTERS, NOT INCLUDING MY FOUR FRIENDS AND SOME STRIPE-TASTIC WALLY-WATCHERS. NOW SEEK OUT THE CHARACTERS WHO MATCH THE SILHOUETTES ABOVE. TRY NOT TO GO OOGLY-BOOGLY-WOOGLY EYED!

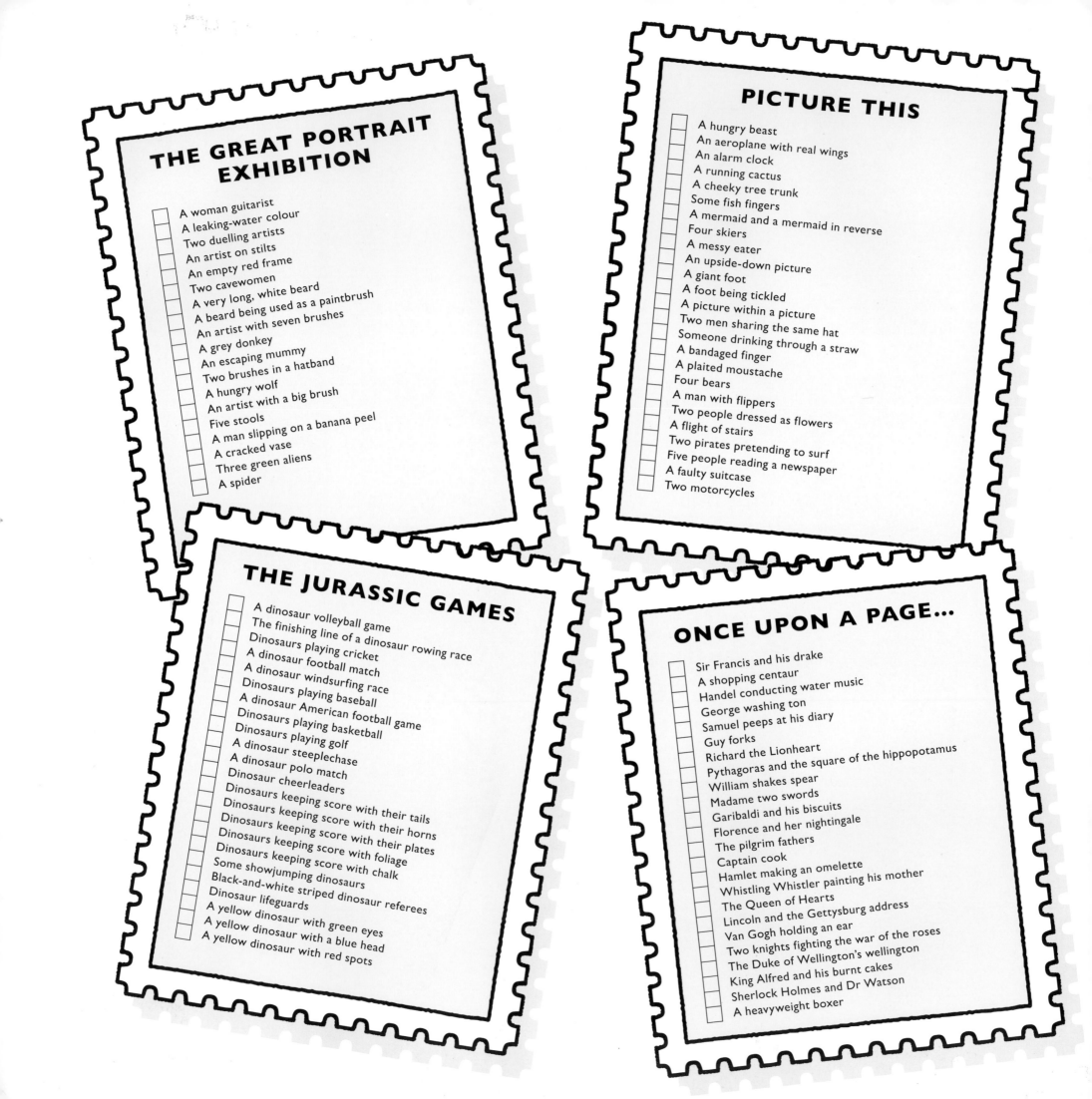

THE GREAT PORTRAIT EXHIBITION

- A woman guitarist
- A leaking-water colour
- Two duelling artists
- An artist on stilts
- An empty red frame
- Two cavewomen
- A very long, white beard
- A beard being used as a paintbrush
- An artist with seven brushes
- A grey donkey
- An escaping mummy
- Two brushes in a hatband
- A hungry wolf
- An artist with a big brush
- Five stools
- A man slipping on a banana peel
- A cracked vase
- Three green aliens
- A spider

PICTURE THIS

- A hungry beast
- An aeroplane with real wings
- An alarm clock
- A running cactus
- A cheeky tree trunk
- Some fish fingers
- A mermaid and a mermaid in reverse
- Four skiers
- A messy eater
- An upside-down picture
- A giant foot
- A foot being tickled
- A picture within a picture
- Two men sharing the same hat
- Someone drinking through a straw
- A bandaged finger
- A plaited moustache
- Four bears
- A man with flippers
- Two people dressed as flowers
- A flight of stairs
- Two pirates pretending to surf
- Five people reading a newspaper
- A faulty suitcase
- Two motorcycles

THE JURASSIC GAMES

- A dinosaur volleyball game
- The finishing line of a dinosaur rowing race
- Dinosaurs playing cricket
- A dinosaur football match
- A dinosaur windsurfing race
- Dinosaurs playing baseball
- A dinosaur American football game
- Dinosaurs playing basketball
- Dinosaurs playing golf
- A dinosaur steeplechase
- A dinosaur polo match
- Dinosaur cheerleaders
- Dinosaurs keeping score with their tails
- Dinosaurs keeping score with their horns
- Dinosaurs keeping score with their plates
- Dinosaurs keeping score with foliage
- Dinosaurs keeping score with chalk
- Some showjumping dinosaurs
- Black-and-white striped dinosaur referees
- Dinosaur lifeguards
- A yellow dinosaur with green eyes
- A yellow dinosaur with a blue head
- A yellow dinosaur with red spots

ONCE UPON A PAGE...

- Sir Francis and his drake
- A shopping centaur
- Handel conducting water music
- George washing ton
- Samuel peeps at his diary
- Guy forks
- Richard the Lionheart
- Pythagoras and the square of the hippopotamus
- William shakes spear
- Madame two swords
- Garibaldi and his biscuits
- Florence and her nightingale
- The pilgrim fathers
- Captain cook
- Hamlet making an omelette
- Whistling Whistler painting his mother
- The Queen of Hearts
- Lincoln and the Gettysburg address
- Van Gogh holding an ear
- Two knights fighting the war of the roses
- The Duke of Wellington's wellington
- King Alfred and his burnt cakes
- Sherlock Holmes and Dr Watson
- A heavyweight boxer

DINOSAURS, SPACEMEN AND GHOULS

- "Hand" luggage
- A fly in a saucer
- A ticklish dinosaur
- A dinosaur dressed as a caveman
- A man on a hanger
- A spaceship
- Stars in a star's dressing room
- A cheeky dinosaur
- A planet picnic
- A game of hoopla
- A wolfman having a howling good time
- A spacecastle
- Two people reading books
- Four cavemen going up in the world
- Seven red caps
- Two bottles of ketchup
- Two fish in helmets
- Shelves of giant portions
- A vampire with no reflection in his mirror
- Four mummies
- A vulture

THE CAKE FACTORY

- A loading bay
- A man juggling eggs
- Two Danish pastries
- A gingerbread man
- Two workers blowing cream horns
- Maple syrup
- Hot cross buns
- A Viennese whirl
- A Swiss roll
- A pan cake
- A chocolate moose
- A custard-pie fight
- Apple pie
- Black forest gateau
- A cake with a bite out of it
- Rock cakes
- Two kinds of dough nuts
- A doe nut
- Baked Alaska pudding
- A fairy cake
- Mississippi mud pie
- Carrot cake
- A tea cake
- A teapot cake
- Sprinkles

THE WILD WILD WEST

- Two cowboys about to draw against each other
- Drinkers raising their glasses to a lady
- Outlaws holding up a stagecoach
- Some boisterous cowboys painting the town red
- Doc holiday
- The film wardrobe department
- Buffalo Bill
- The loan ranger
- Gamblers playing cards
- A couple of gunslingers
- Calamity Jane
- A buffalo stampede
- A spaghetti western
- A horse-drawn wagon
- Billy the kid
- Townspeople saluting General Store
- A band of outlaws
- A surrendering cactus
- A tethered horse and its rider
- A horse being shoed
- A jail break
- Eleven bags of money
- A skunk
- Two cowboys shouting "This town ain't big enough for the both of us."

THE GREAT ESCAPE

- Ten men wearing a green hood
- Ten men wearing only one glove
- Ten men wearing two different coloured gloves
- Ten men wearing short and long gloves
- Ten lost gloves
- Ten men wearing one fingerless glove
- Six ladders
- Nineteen shovels
- A skeleton
- A set of traffic lights
- Three rockets
- Two birds
- A cannon
- Three helicopter helmets
- A rabbit
- Seven red-and-yellow flags
- Four balloons
- A sign pointing up
- Three sets of man-made wings
- Eleven white handkerchiefs
- A walking stick
- Smoke signals
- A sling-shot

TOYS! TOYS! TOYS!

- A kangaroo in a pouch
- A fish tank
- Four baby's bottles
- Two anchors
- A toy figure on skis
- A chalkboard
- A toy figure pushing a wheelbarrow
- A crow's nest
- An apple tree bookend
- A dog playing the cymbals
- Five big red books
- A toy performer balancing two chairs in the air
- Five wooden ladders
- A giraffe with a red-and-white striped scarf
- A magnifying glass
- A pirate carrying a barrel
- Toy figures climbing up a long scarf
- A teddy bear with a bow tie
- A crossing guard tied up at work
- A yellow umbrella and a pink umbrella
- A toy chick carrying an egg
- A red toy planet
- A chain of villains
- A frog prince

PIRATE PANORAMA

- A school of whales
- A giant wave
- A pirate riding the serf
- Two birds
- Seven flags
- A pirate walking the plank
- A pirate with his trousers down
- The deep blue C
- Two sharks
- A pirate with an axe and a cutlass
- A tap
- Four cannon balls
- A two-foot gun barrel
- Four golden chalices
- A person-shaped hole
- A crow's nest
- A pirate with a hook
- A pirate in love
- A sinking island

THE DRAGON FLYERS

- Two dragons on a collision course
- A pedestrian crossing
- Ten yellow dragons
- Two pairs of hitchhikers
- Salesmen selling young dragons
- Dragon flyer highwaymen
- A concussed dragon
- Dragon cops and robbers
- Three dragons flying upside down
- A dragon beauty parlour
- A flying tower
- A dragon-tail staircase
- A topsy-turvy tower
- An upside-down tower
- Dragons in love
- Flyers with dragon-tail-shaped beards
- A dragon rider covering his eyes
- A tail fight
- A passenger with empty pockets
- Queues at three bus dragon stops
- One person wearing two red shoes
- A dragon flying backwards
- A dragon indoors

THE LAND OF WALLIES

- A blue-and-white bobble hat
- Wallies standing still
- Wallies giving the thumbs-up
- Wallies looking frightened
- Wallies lying down
- Wallies being chased
- Wallies with bobble hats
- Wallies without bobble hats
- Wallies raising their bobble hats
- Wallies with walking sticks
- Wallies without walking sticks
- Wallies with spectacles
- Wallies without spectacles
- Wallies with pockets
- Wallies without pockets
- A Wally holding a wing
- Wallies searching
- A chair
- A sword
- A kettle
- A blue vase
- A snorkle
- A bird

ONE LAST THING...

Did you find Wally's globe in one of the scenes? If not, then keep on searching!

ONE VERY LAST THING...

Look closely at the front and back pages. One stamp of each character is not like the others. Can you spot the odd ones out?